Rhinegold Study Guides

Listening Tests for Students

Edexcel GCSE Music Specification

Book 4

by

Jim Harrison and Simon Rushby

Rhinegold Publishing Ltd
239–241 Shaftesbury Avenue
London WC2H 8TF
Telephone: 020 7333 1720
Fax: 020 7333 1765
www.rhinegold.co.uk

Music Study Guides

GCSE, AS and A2 Music Study Guides (AQA, Edexcel and OCR)
GCSE, AS and A2 Music Listening Tests (AQA, Edexcel and OCR)
GCSE Music Study Guide (WJEC)
GCSE Music Listening Tests (WJEC)
AS/A2 Music Technology Study Guide (Edexcel)
AS/A2 Music Technology Listening Tests (Edexcel)
Revision Guides for GCSE (AQA, Edexcel and OCR), AS and A2 Music (AQA and Edexcel)

Also available from Rhinegold Education

Key Stage 3 Elements
Key Stage 3 Listening Tests: Book 1 and Book 2
AS and A2 Music Harmony Workbooks
GCSE and AS Music Composition Workbooks
GCSE and AS Music Literacy Workbooks
Romanticism in Focus, Baroque Music in Focus, Film Music in Focus, Modernism in Focus,
The Immaculate Collection in Focus, *Who's Next* in Focus, *Batman* in Focus, *Goldfinger* in Focus,
Musicals in Focus

Rhinegold also publishes Choir & Organ, Classical Music, Classroom Music, Early Music Today,
International Piano, Music Teacher, Opera Now, Piano, The Singer, Teaching Drama,
British and International Music Yearbook, British Performing Arts Yearbook,
British Music Education Yearbook, Rhinegold Dictionary of Music in Sound

Other Rhinegold Study Guides

Rhinegold publishes resources for candidates studying Drama and Theatre Studies.

First published 2007 in Great Britain by
Rhinegold Publishing Limited
239–241 Shaftesbury Avenue
London WC2H 8TF
Telephone: 020 7333 1720
Fax: 020 7333 1765
www.rhinegold.co.uk

© Rhinegold Publishing Limited 2007

Reprinted 2009

All rights reserved. No part of this publication may be reproduced, stored in a retrieval system,
or transmitted in any form or by any means, electronic, mechanical, photocopying, recording or otherwise,
without the prior permission of Rhinegold Publishing Ltd.

This title is excluded from any licence issued by the Copyright Licensing Agency,
or other Reproduction Rights Organisation.
Rhinegold Publishing Ltd has used its best efforts in preparing this guide. It does not assume, and hereby
disclaims, any liability to any party for loss or damage caused by errors or omissions in the guide whether
such errors or omissions result from negligence, accident of other cause.

You should always check the current requirements of the examination, since these may change.
Copies of the Edexcel Specification may be obtained from
Edexcel Examinations at Edexcel Publications, Adamsway, Mansfield, Notts NG18 4FN
Telephone 01623 467467, Fax 01623 450481, email publications@linneydirect.com
See also the Edexcel website at www.edexcel.com

Listening Tests for Students Book 4: Edexcel GCSE Music Specification

British Library Cataloguing in Publication Data.
A catalogue record for this book is available from the British Library.
ISBN: 978-1-906178-21-5
Printed in Great Britain by Headley Brothers Ltd

The authors

Jim Harrison is head of music at the Latymer School, Edmonton. Prior to working in secondary schools he was involved in various areas of music education: lecturing at the Royal Welsh College of Music & Drama; teaching at the University of Birmingham and Royal Holloway College; and tutoring in adult education (composition, contemporary music and string orchestra coaching). Other freelance work has included a range of composition commissions, working as an arranger and copyist for Ray Davies, and working as a statistician for a BBC football commentator. He currently delivers the A-level part of the PGCE course at the Institute of Education and runs A-level and GCSE INSET courses for Keynote Educational. He is also co-author of Rhinegold's *Key Stage 3 Listening Tests* Books 1 and 2, and *Edexcel GCSE Listening Tests: Book 3*. He completed his PhD composition portfolio and thesis in 2002.

Simon Rushby has been teaching music to students aged 11–18 for many years, and is currently director of music at Reigate Grammar School in Surrey, having been director and assistant director of music at three other schools. He has written extensive study guides for GCSE and A-level Music for the Naxos Music Library, and has also been a principal examiner for A-level Music. Simon is also busy as a conductor and performer, and is a published songwriter and composer of production music for TV and film.

Editors

Lucien Jenkins, Chris Elcombe, Emma Findlow, Rose Vickridge, Katherine Smith and Sophie Buchan. The authors would also like to thank Alec Boulton for his invaluable help in producing the CD.

Compact disc

A CD containing recordings of all the extracts for the listening tests in this book is available from Rhinegold, tel 020 7333 1720, fax 020 7333 1765, email sales@rhinegold.co.uk, or order online at www.rhinegold.co.uk.

Copyright acknowledgements

The publishers and authors are grateful to the following publishers for permission to use printed excerpts from their publications:

Love Can't Turn Around: Words and music by Isaac Hayes © Copyright 1994 Incense Production Incorporated. Prestige Music Limited. Used by permission of Music Sales Limited. All rights reserved. International copyright secured.

Sally Cinnamon: Words and music by John Squire & Ian Brown © Copyright 1987 Zomba Music Publishers Limited. Used by permission of Music Sales Limited. All rights reserved. International copyright secured.

Sunny Afternoon: Words and music by Ray Davies © Copyright 1966 Davray Music Limited. Carlin Music Corporation. Used by permission of Music Sales Limited. All rights reserved. International copyright secured.

Symphony Op 21: Copyright 1929 by Universal Edition. Copyright renewed 1956 by Anton Webern's Erben. Reproduced by permission. All rights reserved.

You'd Be So Nice to Come Home to: Words and music by Cole Porter © 1942 Chappell Co Inc. Warner/Chappell Music Ltd, London W6 8BS. Reproduced by permission of Faber Music Ltd. All rights reserved.

The authors are grateful to the following who have granted permission for the use of their recordings: ARC Music Limited, Chandos, Demon Music Group Limited, Donemus, Graham Fitkin, Haenssler, Kontor, Mark Allan, Nascente, Naxos, Skint, Sony BMG and World Music Network.

Teacher's guide

Answers to all of the questions and full track listings are given in the accompanying *Teacher's Guide*, available from Rhinegold, tel 020 7333 1720, fax 020 7333 1765, email sales@rhinegold.co.uk, or order online at www.rhinegold.co.uk.

Introduction

Rhinegold also publishes Book 1, Book 2 and Book 3 of Listening Tests for Students for the Edexcel GCSE Music Specification (Rhinegold, 2003, 2005 and 2007 respectively).

You will also find it helpful to refer to *A Student's Guide to GCSE Music for Edexcel* (Rhinegold, 2006).

Welcome to Book 4 of Listening Tests for Students for the Edexcel GCSE Music Specification. At the end of your GCSE Music course you will have to sit a Listening and Appraising test. This test lasts for 1½ hours, is worth 40% of the total marks for the exam, and is taken in May or June during the final year of your course. This book is designed to help you get the best possible mark in this test by giving you practice in the different types of question you are likely to come across, and to help you to develop the skills, understanding and knowledge needed to tackle the GCSE examination with confidence.

In the listening test you will have to answer questions based on a selection of recorded extracts. These extracts will be taken from music that relates to the four Areas of Study you will have explored on your course. These Areas of Study are:

➢ Structure in western classical music 1600–1899

➢ Changing directions in western classical music from 1900

➢ Popular music in context

➢ Indian raga, African music and fusions.

The questions in this book have been grouped into the above Areas of Study and on the pages that follow you will find questions that have been designed like the ones you will get in the real examination. In order to answer these you will need to listen to the relevant track on the accompanying CD or listen to them using a legal download site (in a few questions, CD timings have been included to help you identify locations – note that these are not normally given in actual exam papers); these tracks have been chosen to provide clear examples of the musical concepts and styles that you need to know for GCSE Music.

This book isn't just about listening though. One of the main purposes of this book, and indeed of the GCSE course, is to help you to gain a deeper insight into a wide range of music, and to understand how it works. A very good way to do this is to identify specific composing techniques from the music that you listen to, and then experiment with these techniques yourself. This is indeed something you are expected to do as part of your GCSE. There are plenty of models in this book of composers combining musical techniques from very different styles – see questions 18 and 35, for example.

One of the really good things about GCSE Music is the variety of musical styles that it covers. One disadvantage is that the increasing emphasis on more recent music in the syllabus caused us difficulties when collecting the musical examples to accompany this book. Some record labels were unwilling to provide us with permission to use their tracks. As a result we are unable to provide recordings of two of these tracks on the CD, something for which we sincerely apologise. However, these tracks (indicated in the text by the symbol 🎵) can easily be downloaded as individual tracks from sites such as iTunes (www.apple.com/uk/itunes) and Napster (www.napster.co.uk) at a reasonable price.

Aside from these problems, we have enjoyed collecting the musical examples for this book and hope that you will discover new music that you want to explore further, while coming to understand familiar musical styles in more depth. If you really like a particular track, your teacher has a Teacher's Guide that lists where each piece of music is from – your teacher will be able to let you know where to find more of the same kind of music.

Types of question

There are three types of question in the listening tests:

1. General listening questions. These tend to be questions based on your ability to identify musical detail such as instruments and compositional devices, to make comparisons, to complete missing notes in a melody, or to identify a chord or the shape of a musical phrase. The best ways to prepare yourself for this type of question are to study music theory and to develop aural skills by being involved in lots of music-making, especially when this involves singing in parts and/or reading music notation.

2. Questions that require you to relate what you hear to your knowledge of the Areas of Study. In the examination (and in this book) each question starts by telling you which Area of Study it relates to. This type of question might ask you to say how what you hear is characteristic of Indian raga (or another world music tradition that you have studied) or to identify how variation technique has been used in a particular piece. The best way to prepare for this is to listen to lots of music across all of the Areas of Study, and to be able to identify key features from each style of music.

3. Context questions. These questions can be really tricky, as they require you not only to have listened to music but also to understand the background to particular musical styles and the factors that had an impact on the creation of the music. You won't be expected to know specific pieces of music but you might, for example, be expected to show that you understand the varied musical influences on African music. You can prepare for this by researching the context of any music you listen to, as suggested in the table on the right.

To be successful in the listening test then, you will need to combine general listening skills with detailed knowledge of the Areas of Study. How will you know exactly what you need to learn? Edexcel publishes a specification for GCSE Music and this contains details of what you need to know for each Area of Study, as well as a general list of the musical language you should know and be able to recognise. You would be well advised to be thoroughly familiar

Questions to ask yourself about the music that you study:
- How does the music relate to the purpose or context it was created for?
- What are the conventions of this piece of music – what normally happens in music of this style?
- How does the music relate to different cultures or traditions?
- How have the available musical resources been used to create the music?
- How do musical styles and traditions change over time and in different places?

> The musical terms you need to know are explained in *A Student's Guide to GCSE Music* for Edexcel (Rhinegold, 2006), especially in the glossary and in the chapter on 'Understanding Music'. You can also find a list of these terms in the specification. Ask your teacher for a copy, or download your own from the Edexcel website (www.edexcel.com).

with this, and to understand what all of the listed musical words mean before you take the GCSE listening test. Your teacher will have a copy of the specification and can give you this information.

It is not enough, of course, just to know dictionary definitions of musical words and terms – you need to know what they sound like as well so you can recognise them when they appear in different contexts. This is where this book and the CD can really help to support the work you are doing on your GCSE course.

How to use this book

Knowledge and understanding

There are two main ways to use this book and CD: as practice mock-exam material and to develop your knowledge and understanding.

To use this book to develop your skills, read each question carefully before you listen to the extract, and if there are any words that you don't understand, look them up before you go any further. Try the questions but don't worry if you find some of them hard at first, or if you need more playings than are suggested.

Practising for the exam

To practise answering the questions under exam conditions, first select eight recorded extracts – two different topics from each Area of Study. Listen to each recorded extract exactly the number of times stated at the start. Allow yourself 30–60 seconds between each playing, and about two minutes at the end to finish writing your answers.

Some people panic when faced with a recorded examination that only allows a small number of playings for each extract and a time limit for answering. You need to be able to multi-task – you cannot afford to just listen for only one feature on each playing. This is a high-level skill – don't let anybody tell you that GCSE Music is easy! Practising the questions in this book can help you develop effective techniques to use in the exam. Here a few suggestions to help you approach the listening tests:

➢ Read through the question quickly before you hear the music for the first time so you can prepare yourself for what you need to listen for.

➢ Notice that most questions are set out in a logical order; questions about specific parts of the extract come in the order you hear them in, and general questions about the extract as a whole come last. This should help you plan your listening.

➢ Don't try to write your answers out in full while the music is going on, as you will waste valuable listening time. Make rough notes in the margin and write the answers neatly in the pauses after each playing. In the real exam, make sure you put a line through any rough work so that an examiner doesn't mistake this for your final answer.

➢ Don't panic if you are asked to write a description of something but cannot remember the correct name or technical term. Jot down a brief description of what you've heard – there is a good chance the correct name will come back to you later on and you can amend your answer after the final playing.

- Do try to answer all of the questions for each extract. You may find this difficult at first, as it is easy to get bogged down with one particular part. You are more likely to get a good mark by having a go at each question on the extract rather than doing just one section in great detail. In order to give you as much experience of different types of question as possible, some of the extracts in this book have a few more questions than is likely to be the case in the real exam – don't worry if you struggle a bit on the longer questions.

- If you haven't answered all the questions after the last playing, try replaying the piece in your head – the chances are you will be able to remember more about the piece than you think. This can be particularly helpful with the more general type of question, such as context questions.

- In multiple-choice questions, be careful not to select more than the required number of answers (which is often just one). Otherwise you are unlikely to receive a mark, even if one of your answers is correct.

In your GCSE listening exam, many questions can be answered with a single response that, if correct, can earn you one mark. Where they require two or more responses, there will be two or more marks. In the actual exam the marks available for each question will be indicated on the paper.

Marks

In this book you will usually be told if you need to make more than one point in your answer. For example, 'Name two instruments that you can hear' will earn you two marks, 'Give three musical reasons for your choice' will earn you three marks and so on. Questions that require you to add pitches or rhythms usually earn one mark for each note you write, or shape you define. Questions such as these are usually worth a lot of marks (one mark per note quickly adds up) so it is worthwhile practising these.

The answers for all the questions are available in the Teacher's Guide that accompanies the audio CD.

Advice from Edexcel examiners

Every year the Edexcel examiners produce a 'Report on the Examination' that describes how students have done in GCSE music. Your teacher should have a copy of this, but here are a few of the bits of advice the examiners have offered to help you get the best possible mark:

- It is fine for answers to be in short note form, bullet points or sentences.

- You can get good marks either by using correct musical terms or by describing accurately what you hear.

- Concentrate on the question you are answering at the time – don't distract yourself by worrying about whether you got the previous question right. Check how many marks are available for each question and how many responses are required. Be aware that if, for example, you select two options for a multiple-choice question where only one is required, no marks will be awarded.

➢ Avoid vague answers. For example, if you are asked to listen to two similar pieces of music and describe how they are different, an answer such as 'different instruments' won't be enough. To get a good mark you would need to give more detail such as 'strings play melody in first piece – brass play melody in second piece'.

➢ Make sure you are familiar with the key listening words, and with the specific vocabulary for each Area of Study. This will help you to focus your answers and select the relevant information to use.

All that is left to say is good luck in your GCSE exam!

Area of Study 1

The answers for all the questions are available in the Teacher's Guide that accompanies the audio CD.

Ground bass and variations

Question 1 Track 1

Listen to this extract from a passacaglia **four** times and answer the questions below.

An eight-bar theme in the bass part is heard five times in total.

1. What is the name for this compositional technique?

   .... (1)

2. What term describes the texture of the first eight bars?

   .... (1)

3. Complete the missing notes in the bass part. The rhythms have been provided for you.

   (5)

4. Over which of the five statements of the repeating bass line does the following rhythmic idea occur?

   .... (1)

5. What is the term for the musical texture, heard in this extract, in which melodic lines are combined? Put a cross in the correct box.

   Homophony ☒   Modulation ☒   Articulation ☒   Counterpoint ☒   (1)

6. What key is the music in at the start? Use the bass line printed above to help you.

   .... (1)

7. Does the extract remain in the same key throughout the extract?

   .... (1)

[continued overleaf]

10 Area of Study 1: Structure in western classical music 1600–1899

8. The same type of cadence is used at the end of every eight bars. What type of cadence is it? Put a cross in the correct box.

   Perfect ☒   Plagal ☒   Interrupted ☒   Imperfect ☒   (1)

9. Name the instrument featured in this extract.

   .... (1)

10. In which period of music do you think this music was composed?

    .... (1)

(Total 14 marks)

Question 2

Track 2

Listen to the extract **four** times and answer the following questions.

The following theme is used as the basis for variations in this orchestral extract. You will hear the unaccompanied theme, followed by four variations.

1. Underline 'true' or 'false' for each of the following statements.

   a) The theme is diatonic.   True/False

   b) The theme starts with an anacrusis.   True/False

   c) The theme is in simple duple time.   True/False

   d) There is a trill in bar 5.   True/False

   e) The theme has a range of an octave.   True/False   (5)

2. Which section of the orchestra plays variation 1?

   ....
                                                                                                                (1)

3. Describe **one** difference in instrumentation between variations 1 and 2.

   .... (1)

4. In which variation is syncopation used prominently in the accompaniment?

   ....
                                                                                                                (1)

5. In which variation can trills be heard?

   ....
                                                                                                                (1)

6. In the fourth and final variation the theme is fragmented. Which **two** motifs from the theme (labelled a, b, c, d and e on the music above) are used in this variation?

   ....
                                                                                                                (2)

7. Identify the percussion instrument heard in the closing bars of the extract.

   ....
                                                                                                                (1)

(Total 12 marks)

12 Area of Study 1: Structure in western classical music 1600–1899

Question 3 **Track 3**

Listen to the extract **four** times and answer the following questions.

The extract includes a ground bass.

1. The basso continuo in this extract consists of cellos, double basses and which keyboard instrument?

   .... (1)

2. Is this music in a major or minor key?

   .... (1)

3. Does this music have two, three or four beats in a bar?

   .... (1)

4. Fill in the gaps in the sentence below, selecting from the following words:

   | chromatic | pentatonic | trumpet | flute | alto |
   | soprano | descends | clarinet | diatonic | ascends |

   The ground bass consists of a .... scale which .... by step.

   At the start, short regular chords are played by strings and a ...., and the ....

   .... section of the choir enters first with the word 'Crucifixus'. (4)

5. How many complete statements of the ground bass are there before the vocal parts first enter?

   .... (1)

6. What word best describes the texture of the vocal parts in the second half of this extract? Put a cross in the correct box.

   Monophonic ☒   Homophonic ☒   Polyphonic ☒   Heterophonic ☒   (1)

7. Give **three** ways, other than the key, in which the composer achieves a sense of sadness in this music.

   a) ....

   b) ....

   c) .... (3)

8. Identify the musical period in which this piece was written, and give a reason for your answer.

   a) Period: ....

   b) Reason: .... (2)

   (Total 14 marks)

Area of Study 1: Structure in western classical music 1600–1899 13

Ternary form

Question 4

Track 4

Listen to this complete version of *Serenade* by Derek Bourgeois **four** times and answer the following questions.

This piece is in ternary form.

1. What type of ensemble is playing this extract?

   .... (1)

2. Name the melody instrument heard after the short introduction. Put a cross in the correct box.

   Alto saxophone ☒   Cornet ☒   Horn ☒   Muted trumpet ☒   (1)

3. The time signature in the A section sounds as if it alternates between $\frac{6}{8}$ and which of the following? Put a cross in the correct box.

   $\frac{2}{4}$ ☒ $\frac{5}{8}$ ☒ $\frac{3}{4}$ ☒ $\frac{4}{4}$ ☒   (1)

4. Identify **three** musical differences between the A and B sections.

   a) ....

   b) ....

   c) .... (3)

5. Identify **two** ways (other than those outlined in the previous question) in which the A section is altered on its return.

   a) ....

   b) .... (2)

6. Describe how the following musical elements are used to create a sense of finality at the end of the piece.

   a) Dynamics ....

   b) Texture ....

   c) Tempo .... (3)

7. Name **three** percussion instruments heard in this piece.

   a) ....

   b) ....

   c) .... (3)

(Total 14 marks)

14 Area of Study 1: Structure in western classical music 1600–1899

Question 5

Track 5

Listen to 'Polka' from *Three Easy Pieces* by Stravinsky **four** times and answer the questions below.

1. What instrument can you hear in this extract?

   .... (1)

2. What is the time signature of the music? Put a cross in the correct box.

   $\frac{2}{4}$ ☒ $\frac{3}{4}$ ☒ $\frac{6}{8}$ ☒ $\frac{5}{4}$ ☒   (1)

3. Which term best describes the bass part of this extract? Put a cross in the correct box.

   Walking bass ☒   Ostinato ☒   Irregular ☒

   Atonal ☒   Alberti bass ☒   (1)

4. Complete the following summary of the structure of the piece by filling in the blank box.

A (repeated)	B	

   (1)

5. What is the correct term for the form of this piece?

   .... (1)

6. The tempo indication at the start is ♩ = 96. What does this mean?

   .... (1)

7. How does the tempo change at the end of the B section?

   .... (1)

8. What aspect of the music indicates that this was composed in the early 20th century, as opposed to an earlier period?

   .... (1)

   (Total 8 marks)

Question 6

Track 6

Listen to this extract **four** times and answer the questions below.

This extract is in ternary form, and its form can be summarised as follows:

A section | B1 section (violins only) | B2 section | A section

1. This extract features which section of the orchestra?

   .... (1)

2. Complete the opening violin melody below. The rhythm of the missing notes has been given for you.

   (6)

3. The section we have called B1 is for violins only.

   a) Is this section in the same key as the A section?

   .... (1)

   b) What is the interval between the two sets of violins in this section?

   .... (1)

4. For each of the following statements about the B2 section, underline 'true' or 'false' as appropriate.

   a) The B2 section starts in the tonic key.   True/False

   b) The B2 section is in a different time signature to the B1 section.   True/False

   c) The cellos hold a pedal note throughout the B2 section.   True/False

   d) The B2 section ends in the major.   True/False   (4)

5. At some points in this extract rubato is used. What does this term mean?

   .... (1)

6. When the A section returns there are a number of differences from its first playing. Name **two** of these differences.

   a) ....

   b) .... (2)

   (Total 16 marks)

16 Area of Study 1: Structure in western classical music 1600–1899

Rondo form

Question 7   Track 7

Listen to the extract **four** times and answer the questions below.

The extract is technically an example of ritornello form, but the structure of its sections – A B A C A D A – means that it also fits into this 'Rondo form' section very well.

1. What is the technical name given to the B and C sections in a rondo?

   .... (1)

2. To what type of work does this extract belong? Put a cross in the correct box.

   String quartet ☒   Violin sonata ☒   Violin concerto ☒   String symphony ☒   (1)

3. From which movement of a work is this extract most likely to have been taken?

   .... (1)

4. Underline 'true' or 'false' for each of the following statements.

   a) The A sections are all identical in length and content.   True/False

   b) The B section is in a minor key.   True/False

   c) The music has a fast tempo and is in simple triple time.   True/False   (3)

5. Which section includes double stopping near the start?

   .... (1)

6. Which section starts in a minor key?

   .... (1)

7. What period of music is this extract from? Give **two** reasons for your answer.

   a) Period: ....

   b) Reason 1: ....

   Reason 2: .... (3)

8. Name the composer of this music. Put a cross in the correct box.

   Beethoven ☒   Berlioz ☒   Bach ☒   Bartók ☒   (1)

(Total 12 marks)

Question 8

Track 8

Listen to the extract **four** times and answer the questions below.

It is taken from a rondo form movement from a quintet by Mozart. The extract consists of the following sections:

End of B section	A1 section	Start of C section
12 seconds	approx. 20 seconds	approx. 20 seconds

1. The B section ends with a repeated note in the bass. What is this device called?

   .... (1)

2. Below is the main melody from the A1 section. Mark 'tr' above the point where you hear a trill and add the three missing notes (the rhythms have been provided for you).

   (4)

3. What is the key of the A1 section?

   .... (1)

4. What does the symbol ¢ mean?

   .... (1)

Here is the main melody that starts the C section:

5. In which key does the C section (the final section in this extract) start?

   .... (1)

6. What instrument plays this melody?

   .... (1)

7. Identify three of the other four instruments in this quintet.

   a) .... b) .... c) .... (3)

[continued overleaf]

18 Area of Study 1: Structure in western classical music 1600–1899

8. What sections are most likely to precede and follow the extract you have heard? Add the correct letters in the blank spaces below.

	B	A1	C	

(2)

9. When do you think this music was composed? Put a cross in the correct box.

1664 ☒   1724 ☒   1784 ☒   1844 ☒

(1)

(Total 15 marks)

Question 9

Track 9

Listen to the extract **four** times, and answer the following questions. This extract is in rondo form.

1. The musical example below outlines the theme that begins and ends the recurring A section. Notate the rhythm of bar 2 in the space provided on the stave (the pitches do not matter).

   (5)

2. Name the **two** instruments playing in this extract.

   a) .... b) .... (2)

3. The playing of both instruments in this movement could be described as virtuosic. Explain what this term means.

   .... (1)

4. Which Italian word best describes the tempo of this movement? Put a cross in the correct box.

   Adagio ☒   Moderato ☒   Allegro ☒   Accelerando ☒   (1)

5. This movement is part of a larger work. Is it most likely to be the first, second or last movement?

   .... (1)

6. The overall structure of this rondo is ABACA. Underline whether each of the following statements is true or false.

   a) The B section begins in a different key from the A section.   True/False

   b) The B section includes double stopping.   True/False

   c) The B section ends in a minor key.   True/False

   d) The C section begins in a major key.   True/False

   e) The final A section is followed by a short coda.   True/False   (5)

7. Was this piece written in the Baroque, Classical or Romantic period?

   .... (1)

   (Total 16 marks)

Area of Study 2

Expressionism and serialism

Question 10   Track 10

Listen to the extract **three** times and answer the questions below.

1. This extract is by a composer from the Second Viennese School. Name the three main composers associated with this group.

    a) .... b) .... c) .... (3)

2. From which sort of work is this extract taken? Put a cross in the correct box.

    Opera ☒   Mass ☒   Oratorio ☒   Musical ☒   (1)

3. What compositional device is used in the instrumental writing at the start of the extract? Put a cross in the correct box.

    Sequence ☒   Call and response ☒   Decoration ☒   Imitation ☒   (1)

4. What type of voice can you hear in this extract?

    .... (1)

5. Describe **four** features of the vocal writing in this extract.

    a) ....

    b) ....

    c) ....

    d) .... (4)

6. Comment on the tempo and texture of the music.

    a) Tempo ....

    b) Texture .... (2)

7. In which decade do you think this piece of music was completed? Put a cross in the correct box.

    1820s ☒   1870s ☒   1920s ☒   1970s ☒   (1)

(Total 13 marks)

Area of Study 2: Changing directions in western classical music from 1900 21

Question 11

Track 11

Listen to the extract **three** times and answer the following questions.

This extract uses serial technique.

1. The note row for this piece is heard in its entirety at the start of the extract. The pitches of the row in its prime order are printed below, with the final note (heard on the clarinet) missing:

   B – B♭ – D – E♭ – G – F♯ – G♯ – E – F – C – C♯ –

   What is the pitch of the missing final note?

   ....
   (1)

2. The first three pitches of the inverted version of the row are B – C – G♯. What are the next **three** pitches?

   ....
   (3)

3. Name **three** instruments that you can hear in this extract (apart from clarinet).

   a) .... b) ....

   c) ....
   (3)

4. Verticalisation is used in this music. Explain the meaning of this term.

   .... (1)

5. What is the relevance of the term 'pointillism' to this music?

   ....

   .... (1)

6. Which one of the following is used in this extract? Put a cross in the correct box.

   Cadence ☒   Trill ☒   Drone ☒   Pizzicato ☒   (1)

(Total 10 marks)

Question 12

Track 12

Listen to the extract, which is written using serial techniques, **three** times, and answer the questions below.

1. List **four** musical characteristics of serialism that can be heard in this extract.

   a) ....

   b) ....

   c) ....

   d) .... (4)

2. Put a cross in the box next to the word that best describes the tonality of this extract.

   Major ☒   Minor ☒   Atonal ☒   Modal ☒   (1)

3. The very opening of the extract is mainly for instruments from which section of the orchestra?

   .... (1)

4. After this opening section, which section of the orchestra takes over with faster rhythms?

   .... (1)

5. Which instrument plays the very last note of the extract?

   .... (1)

6. The following Italian terms describe events that occur in this extract. Briefly explain what each word means.

   a) Pizzicato: ....

   b) Ritenuto: ....

   c) Sforzando: .... (3)

7. The note row in this piece in its prime order is printed below.

   On the blank stave below, complete the note row in its inverted form.

   (3)

8. Name a possible composer and year of composition for this extract.

   a) Composer: .... b) Year: .... (2)

   (Total 16 marks)

Minimalism

Question 13 Track 13

Listen to the extract **three** times and answer the questions below.

1. What type of percussion instrument can you hear in this extract? Put a cross in the correct box.

   Gong ☒   Cymbal ☒   Tubular bell ☒   Triangle ☒   (1)

2. Apart from this percussion instrument, what is the name of the type of ensemble in the extract?

   .... (1)

3. Which adjective best describes this music? Put a cross in the correct box.

   Minimalist ☒   Expressionist ☒   Electronic ☒   Experimental ☒   (1)

4. Delete the incorrect words (one of the two words in each box) to complete this sentence:

   Ascending / Descending major / modal scales / triads are played, with instruments moving at different / identical rates, creating a homophonic / polyphonic texture and creating a sense of consonance / dissonance . (6)

5. Comment on both the sense of pulse and the tempo of the music.

   a) Sense of pulse: ....

   b) Tempo: .... (2)

6. Who do you think composed this music? Put a cross in the correct box.

   John Cage ☒   Arvo Pärt ☒   Karlheinz Stockhausen ☒   Alban Berg ☒   (1)

   (Total 12 marks)

24 Area of Study 2: Changing directions in western classical music from 1900

Question 14 Track 14

Listen to the extract from *Hoketus* by Louis Andriessen **three** times, and answer the questions below.

The instrumentation of this piece consists of two identical groups of instruments positioned on either side of the stage. The two ensembles never play at the same time as one another.

1. How can this spatial effect be reproduced on an audio recording?

   .... (1)

2. Identify **two** instruments you can hear.

   a) ....

   b) .... (2)

3. Do you think this piece belongs in the 'minimalism' or the 'experimental music' part of the GCSE course, or both? Give **three** reasons in your answer.

   ....

   ....

   .... (3)

4. What **further** musical evidence is there that this music was composed in the last 50 years? Give **two** reasons in your answer.

   ....

   .... (2)

(Total 8 marks)

Question 15 Track 15

Listen to this extract **four** times, and answer the questions below.

1. Which section of the orchestra is playing in this extract?

   .... (1)

2. Which term best describes the texture of the opening 10 seconds? Put a cross in the correct box.

   Monophonic ☒   Homophonic ☒   Heterophonic ☒   Polyphonic ☒   (1)

3. After 10 seconds a second part enters at what interval above the first part? Put a cross in the correct box.

   3rd ☒   4th ☒   5th ☒   7th ☒   (1)

4. Towards the end of the extract, which playing technique can be heard? Put a cross in the correct box.

   Pizzicato ☒   Col legno ☒   Harmonics ☒   Double-stopping ☒   (1)

5. Underline the **one** correct statement below.

   The extract begins and ends with slowly formed major triads.

   The extract begins and ends with slowly formed minor triads.

   The extract begins with a slowly formed major triad and ends with a minor triad.

   The extract begins with a slowly formed minor triad and ends with a major triad. (1)

6. Describe as accurately as you can the main rhythmic and dynamic features in this extract. Make at least **two** points about each.

   a) Rhythm: ....

   ....

   ....

   b) Dynamics: ....

   ....

   .... (4)

[continued overleaf]

26 Area of Study 2: Changing directions in western classical music from 1900

7. Identify **three** features of minimalist music heard in this extract.

   a) ....

   b) ....

   c) .... (3)

8. Name a possible composer of this extract.

   .... (1)

   (Total 13 marks)

Experimental and electronic music

Question 16 Track 16

Listen to the extract by George Antheil **three** times and answer the following questions.

1. What section of the orchestra dominates this music?

   .... (1)

2. Name **two pitched** instruments and **two unpitched** instruments that you can hear in this extract.

   a) Pitched: .... and ....

   b) Unpitched: .... and .... (4)

3. Comment on the composer's use of dynamics in this extract. Make **three** points in your answer.

   ....

   ....

   .... (3)

4. Which of the following best describes the metre or time signature(s) used? Put a cross in the correct box.

   Simple triple ☒   Compound duple ☒

   No time signatures used ☒   Irregular and varied ☒ (1)

5. Which **three** features can you hear in the music? Put a cross in each of the correct boxes.

   Double-stopping ☒   Note cluster ☒   Multi-tracking ☒

   Atonality ☒   Pedal ☒   Dissonance ☒ (3)

   (Total 12 marks)

28 Area of Study 2: Changing directions in western classical music from 1900

Question 17

Track 17

Listen to the extract of music from a piece by Graham Fitkin **three** times, and answer the following questions.

The extract combines features of electronic music, experimental music, minimalism and dance music. A performance of this work involves two musicians, a video technician and projection equipment.

1. What is the orchestral instrument heard in this extract?

   .... (1)

2. Which of the following features can you hear in the music? Write a tick in the 'Yes' or 'No' column for each feature.

	Yes	No
Sustained chords		
Bass riff		
Off-beat hi-hat		
Broken chords		
Middle eight		
Continuo		

   (6)

3. Identify **two** aspects of this extract that show the influence of modern dance music.

   a) ....

   b) .... (2)

4. Name **two** pieces of electronic music equipment that would be needed for this music to be performed.

   a) ....

   b) .... (2)

5. In general over the course of the extract, how do the following aspects of the music change?

   a) Dynamics: ....

   b) Texture: .... (2)

6. Identify **two** aspects of this composition that could be regarded as 'experimental'.

   a) ....

   b) .... (2)

   (Total 15 marks)

Question 18

Track 18

This extract is from a piece composed in 1968 for six amplified voices.
Listen to it **three** times and answer the questions below.

1. Some aspects of this piece are left for the performers to determine. Give **two** likely examples of aspects that the **composer** has determined.

   a) ....

   b) .... (2)

2. This music is sung *a cappella*. What does this mean?

   .... (1)

The two words 'Vishnu' and 'Elyon' are called out by a soprano and a baritone respectively in the middle of the extract.

3. Describe how 'Vishnu' is treated by the vocal group once the soloist has called it for the first time. You should include **two** points in your answer.

   ....

   .... (2)

4. What is the interval between the two lowest voices just after 'Vishnu' is heard for the first time?

   .... (1)

5. After 'Elyon' is called out, the bass voice uses the word repetitively. Which of the following is the most accurate notation of the rhythm of this repetition? Put a cross in the correct box.

   (1)

6. Give a title and a composer of an experimental piece for voices that you have studied.

   a) Title: ....   b) Composer: ....

   (2)

   (Total 9 marks)

Area of Study 3

Dance music 1985 – present day

Question 19 Track 19

Listen to this dance track – *Love Can't Turn Around* by Farley 'Jackmaster' Funk – **four** times, and answer the following questions.

1. Is this song in a major or minor key?

   .... (1)

2. Identify the rhythmic feature heard in the finger click sound at the start of this extract.

   .... (1)

3. Place a cross in the box alongside the correct notation of the opening line of the song's vocals.

   ☒
   ☒
   ☒
   ☒ (1)

4. Name the part of the drum kit that enters at the words 'They say we were…' (at 00:16 in the extract).

   .... (1)

5. At the part when the kick drum and keyboard 'hits' enter (after the words of the title are heard), panning is used. Explain as precisely as you can what 'panning' means.

   ....
   .... (2)

6. When the singer re-enters, how does what he sings differ from the previous verse (apart from the lyrics)? Make **two** points in your answer.

   a) ....

   b) .... (2)

7. This is an example of house music. Identify **four** characteristics of house that can be heard in this extract.

   a) ....

   b) ....

   c) ....

   d) .... (4)

8. In which city in the USA did house music originate?

   .... (1)

(Total 13 marks)

Question 20

Track 20

Listen to the extract from *9 PM (Till I Come)* by atb **four** times, and answer the questions below.

Though '9 PM' is generally known as a trance track, atb is a German artist and the track contains a number of techno characteristics.

1. List **four** characteristics of techno heard in this track.

    a) ....

    b) ....

    c) ....

    d) .... (4)

2. When the bass sound enters, is it playing on or off the beat?

    .... (1)

3. What term describes the kick drum part in this extract?

    .... (1)

4. Identify and describe the specific studio technique that has created the female voice interjections in this extract.

    a) Name of technique: .... (1)

    b) Description: ....

    .... (1)

5. What effect is added to the sound of the female voice?

    .... (1)

6. After about a minute, a chordal synthesiser riff is added. What is the interval between the two notes in this repeated chord?

    .... (1)

7. Put a cross in the box of the correct rhythm for this synthesiser riff.

    (1)

(Total 11 marks)

Question 21   Track 21

Listen to the extract of *Praise You* by Fatboy Slim **three** times, and answer the questions below.

1. What is the tempo of this track? Put a cross in the correct box.

   60 bpm ☒   90 bpm ☒   110 bpm ☒   140 bpm ☒   (1)

2. The piano plays a repeated chord sequence through almost the entire extract. Which one of the following statements is true? Underline your answer.

   All the chords are major.

   All the chords are minor.

   There is at least one major chord and at least one minor chord   (1)

3. Describe **two** types of sound other than the piano in the opening eight bars of the extract.

   a) ....

   b) ....   (2)

4. In bar 9 the vocals enter. What happens to the final syllable of the phrase 'like I should'?

   .... (1)

5. When the percussion enters, which instrument plays constant semiquavers?

   ....
                                                                                        (1)

6. After the breakdown, which part of the drum kit takes over these semiquavers?

   ....
                                                                                        (1)

7. Describe as precisely as you can what the bass guitar plays when it enters.

   ....

   .... (2)

8. Give **two** reasons why this music is suitable for dancing.

   a) ....

   b) .... (2)

                                                                            (Total 11 marks)

34 Area of Study 3: Popular music in context

Songs from musicals

Question 22

Track 22

Listen to this extract from Cole Porter's song *You'd Be so Nice to Come Home to* **five** times, and answer the questions below.

1. What instruments are playing the rising scale at the start of the extract?

   .... (1)

2. Name the type of voice heard in this extract.

   .... (1)

3. What device can be heard in the upper strings part and the bass part during the first two lines of the vocals?

   .... (1)

4. The verse can be divided into two halves, one beginning when the singer is heard for the first time and the other with the words 'You're not worth...' (at 00:20 in the extract). Name **three** musical differences between these two halves.

   a) ....

   b) ....

   c) .... (3)

5. The chorus begins with the words of the title (at 00:33 in the extract). Is the tonality major or minor at this point?

   .... (1)

6. Describe the music played by the saxophones during the line that begins 'While the breeze...' (at 00:46). Make **two** points.

   a) ....

   b) .... (2)

7. Which instruments play a countermelody during the line that begins 'Under stars ...' (at 01:00)?

   .... (1)

8. Insert the four missing notes for the line that begins 'To come home...' at the end of the extract. Write your answer onto the score below (the rhythms have been provided for you).

   To come home   [etc.] (4)

(Total 14 marks)

Question 23 Track 23

This duet – 'Sun and Moon' from *Miss Saigon* – is sung by the characters Kim and Chris. Listen to it **four** times and answer the following questions.

1. Name the **two** instruments that play in the introduction to this song.

    a) ....

    b) .... (2)

2. Is this song in a major or a minor key?

    .... (1)

3. What device can be heard in the bass part from the beginning of the extract up to the line that begins 'Joined by...'?

    .... (1)

4. Which tuned percussion instrument can be heard towards the end of Kim's first verse?

    .... (1)

5. How does the orchestral texture change in Chris's first verse?

    ....

    .... (2)

6. How does Chris's vocal melody change for the line that begins 'I'm from a world...' (at 00:56 in the extract)? You should include **two** points in your answer.

    ....

    .... (2)

7. Name or describe the cadence at Chris's next line, beginning 'From all that...' (at 01:03 in the extract).

    .... (1)

8. The whole duet section starting at 'Outside, day starts...' (at 01:21) builds to a climax when the characters sing simultaneously for the first time. Describe **five** ways in which this build-up is achieved in the music.

    a) ....

    b) ....

    c) ....

    d) ....

    e) .... (5)

(Total 15 marks)

Question 24

Track 24

Listen to the extract **three** times, then answer the following questions. The extract is taken from 'Happy Talk', a song from the musical *South Pacific*.

1. What section of the orchestra is used in the introduction?

   .... (1)

2. What playing technique is used in the introduction?

   .... (1)

3. What is the tonality of the extract?

   .... (1)

4. Which rhythm best represents the first four bars of the vocal melody? Put a cross in the correct box

   (1)

5. What is the rhyme scheme of the lyrics in this section? Put a cross in the correct box.

   ABAB ☒   ABCB ☒   ABBA ☒   ABBC ☒   (1)

6. How does the key of the 'Talk about the Moon' section compare with the opening 'Happy Talk' section? Underline the correct answer.

   The 'Talk about the Moon' section is in a higher key than the 'Happy Talk' section.

   The 'Talk about the Moon' section is in a lower key than the 'Happy Talk' section.

   The 'Talk about the Moon' section is major and the 'Happy Talk' section is minor.

   Both sections are in the same major key (1)

7. The following sentence describes the melodic movement of the 'Talk about the Moon' section. Delete the incorrect word(s) from each box as necessary.

   The melody starts with a repeated phrase consisting of ascending / descending steps / leaps, followed by alternating pitches a minor 3rd / perfect 4th apart. (3)

8. This song was composed by Richard Rodgers with the lyrics by Oscar Hammerstein II. Name **one** other famous composer-lyricist partnership associated with musicals.

   .... (2)

9. When do you think this musical was composed? Put a cross in the correct box.

   1910–1929 ☒   1940–1959 ☒   1970–1989 ☒ (1)

   (Total 12 marks)

Britpop and its influences

Question 25 Track 25

Listen to the extract from *Beautiful Ones* by Suede **four** times, and answer the following questions.

1. Which **two** words best fit the introduction of this extract? Put a cross in the appropriate boxes.

   Clean ☒   Distortion ☒   Flange ☒   Riff ☒

   Swing rhythm ☒   Sequence ☒   Keyboards ☒   (2)

2. Put a cross next to the chord progression that is heard throughout the introduction and verse.

   C–D–G–C ☒   C–F–G–G ☒   C–D–F–G ☒   C–D–F–E ☒   (1)

3. Apart from electric guitar and voice, name **three** other instruments that can be heard in this extract.

   a) .... b) ....

   c) .... (3)

4. On which line of the verse does the music of the introduction return? Put a cross in the correct box.

   First ☒   Second ☒   Third ☒   Fourth ☒   (1)

5. Describe as fully as you can what happens in the music at the end of the chorus (at 01:18 in the extract), before the second verse begins. You should make **three** points.

   ....

   ....

   .... (3)

6. What major structural difference is there between the second verse and the first verse?

   .... (1)

7. After the second chorus the music moves into a bridge section (beginning with the words 'You don't think…'). Does this section use the chord progression of the verse or the chorus?

   .... (1)

   (Total 12 marks)

Question 26

Listen to the beginning of *Sally Cinnamon* by The Stone Roses (up to 01:50) **four** times and answer the questions below.

1. Complete the melody of the opening guitar riff on the stave below. The rhythms of the missing notes have been provided for you.

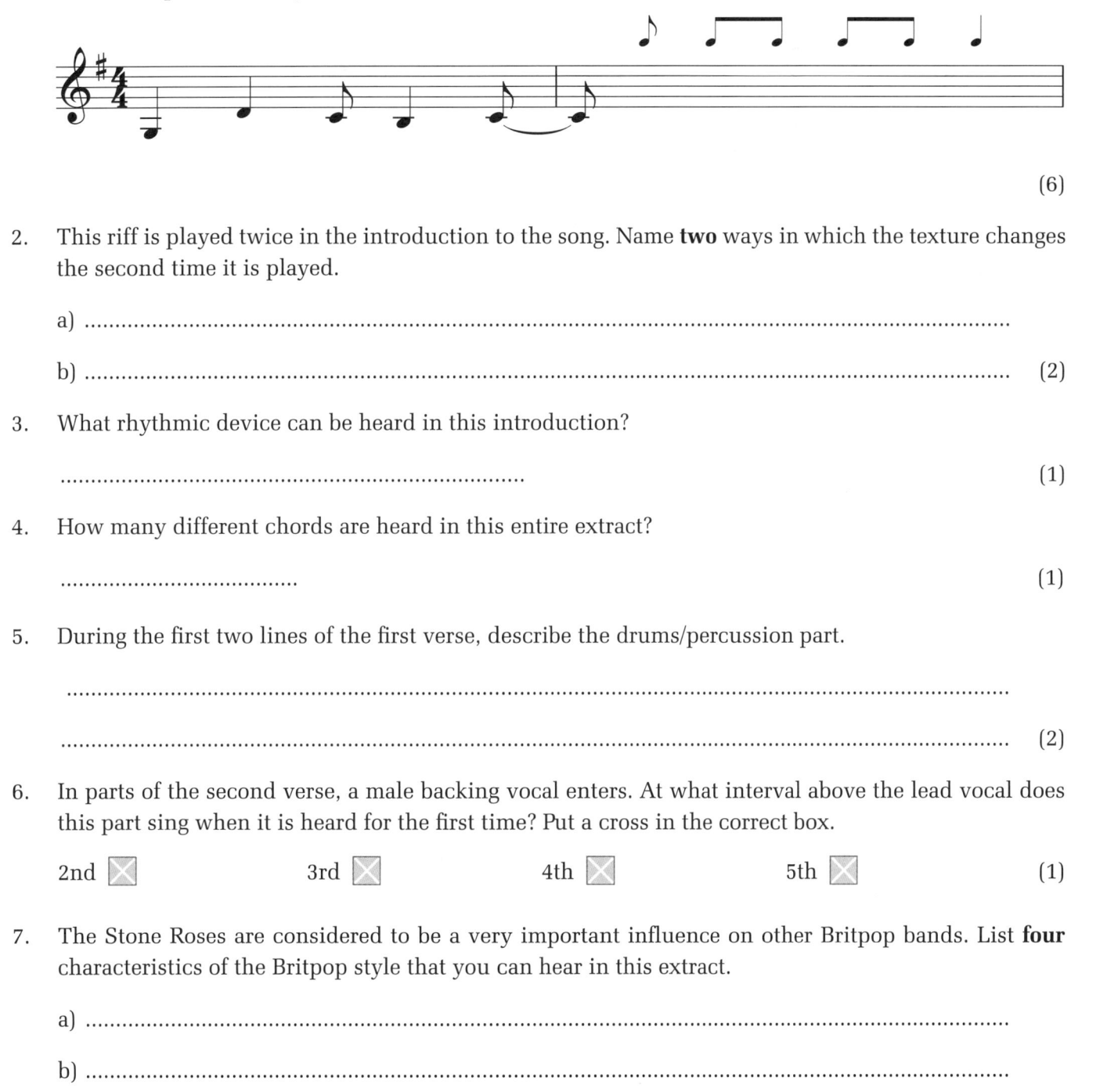

   (6)

2. This riff is played twice in the introduction to the song. Name **two** ways in which the texture changes the second time it is played.

   a) ....

   b) .... (2)

3. What rhythmic device can be heard in this introduction?

   ....

   (1)

4. How many different chords are heard in this entire extract?

   ....

   (1)

5. During the first two lines of the first verse, describe the drums/percussion part.

   ....

   .... (2)

6. In parts of the second verse, a male backing vocal enters. At what interval above the lead vocal does this part sing when it is heard for the first time? Put a cross in the correct box.

   2nd ☒   3rd ☒   4th ☒   5th ☒   (1)

7. The Stone Roses are considered to be a very important influence on other Britpop bands. List **four** characteristics of the Britpop style that you can hear in this extract.

   a) ....

   b) ....

   c) ....

   d) .... (4)

   (Total 17 marks)

40 Area of Study 3: Popular music in context

Question 27

Listen to *Sunny Afternoon*, a track by 1960s band The Kinks, **four** times, and answer the questions below.

1. What is the rhythm of the snare drum fill in bar 4 (the first bar in which the drum kit plays)? Put a cross in the correct box.

    i) ☒   ii) ☒

    iii) ☒   iv) ☒

    v) ☒
    (1)

2. Which of the following best describes the bass part in the introduction? Put a cross in the correct box.

    Descending major scale ☒   Descending chromatic scale ☒

    Ascending minor scale ☒   None of these ☒
    (1)

3. What rhythmic device is used in the melody for the lyrics 'all my dough' (at 00:18 on the recording)?

    ....
    (1)

4. Describe the melodic movement for the lyrics 'sunny afternoon' (when heard for the first time at 00:27). How does this compare to the bass part in the introduction?

    ....

    ....
    (2)

5. Identify **three** instruments used in this track, excluding voice and drum kit.

    a) .... b) ....

    c) ....
    (3)

6. What is the interval between the two vocal parts each time the word 'summertime' is heard? Put a cross in the correct box.

    3rd ☒   4th ☒   5th ☒   Octave ☒
    (1)

7. What is the tempo of this track? Put a cross in the correct box.

    ♩ = 66 ☒   ♩ = 96 ☒   ♩ = 126 ☒   ♩ = 176 ☒
    (1)

8. Outline three ways in which Britpop bands such as Oasis were influenced by tracks like *Sunny Afternoon*.

    a) ....

    b) ....

    c) ....
    (3)

    (Total 13 marks)

Area of Study 4

Indian raga

Question 28 Track 26

Listen to this extract **three** times and answer the following questions.

1. What is the name of the instrument that plays the melodic material throughout this extract?

   .... (1)

2. The extract is taken from the opening of a raga performance. What name is given to this opening section?

   .... (1)

3. List **three** characteristics that you can hear which are typical of the opening section of a raga.

   a) ....

   b) ....

   c) .... (3)

4. Another instrument is present providing a drone for the melodic instrument. What is the most likely name of this drone instrument?

   .... (1)

5. Describe the main characteristics of a raga and its performance. You should make **five** points in your answer.

   ....

   ....

   ....

   ....

   .... (5)

   (Total 11 marks)

Question 29

Track 27

Listen to this extract **three** times and answer the questions below.

1. Name **two** instruments heard in this extract.

   a) ....

   b) .... (2)

2. This extract is part of the 'jhala' section of the raga performance. At what point in a raga performance would this section be heard?

   .... (1)

3. What characteristics of the jhala section can be heard in this extract? You should include **two** points in your answer.

   ....

   .... (2)

4. Which of the following repeating rhythms can be heard in the accompaniment of this extract? Put a cross in the correct box.

   (1)

5. The performer on this track, Irshad Khan, has spent much time playing and teaching in the West. Name **two** aspects of this raga performance that could be described as similar to Western musical characteristics.

   a) ....

   b) .... (2)

6. Describe what happens in the music at the very end of the extract. You should include **three** points in your answer.

   ....

   ....

   .... (3)

7. Explain as precisely as you can what is meant by the following terms, all to do with the tal.

   a) Teental: ....

   ....

   b) Sam: ....

   ....

   c) Matras: ....

   ....

   d) Theka: ....

   .... (4)

   (Total 15 marks)

Question 30

Listen to this extract of Indian music **three** times and answer the questions below.

It involves two instruments. One instrument plays throughout and the other enters after about eight seconds.

1. Tick **one** box in each row to indicate which features are present on the instruments heard in the extract.

	Both instruments	One instrument	Neither instrument
Is / are plucked			
Has / have frets			
Has / have sympathetic strings			

   (3)

2. Complete the two sentences below using words from the following list.

sarod	sarangi	teental	drone
sitar	tanpura	tabla	violin
rag	tal		

   a) The instrument that plays throughout is a .... and its role is to provide an accompaniment called a ....

   b) The melody instrument is a .... and improvises using notes from the ....

   (4)

3. 'Meend' is used in this extract. What do you understand by this term?

   .... (1)

4. From which section of music do you think this music comes? Put a cross in the correct box.

   Jor ☒   Gat ☒   Jhala ☒   Alap ☒   (1)

5. Give **one** reason for your answer to the previous question.

   .... (1)

   (Total 10 marks)

African music

Question 31 Track 29

Listen to this extract **four** times and answer the questions below.

This is a piece of music from Mali. It can be seen to have a structure roughly as follows:

Introduction | Interlude | Verse 1 | Interlude | Verse 2

1. What is the instrument accompanying the singer? Put a cross in the correct box.

   Djembe ☒   Mbira ☒   Kora ☒   Balophon ☒   (1)

2. Underline 'true' or 'false' for each of the statements below.

   a) The introduction is for voice only.   True/False

   b) In the introduction the instrument plays major triads.   True/False

   c) The opening phrase is played four times.   True/False

   d) The introduction contains a pedal note.   True/False   (4)

3. After this introduction, the instrument plays an interlude with a repeated pattern that continues throughout the sung verse.

   a) What is an African name that you have learned for this kind of repeated pattern?

   ....   (1)

   b) Name **one** way in which this pattern is slightly varied before the singer enters.

   ....   (1)

4. After a brief instrumental interlude, the voice returns for the second verse. Name **two** ways in which the vocal melody is different from the first verse.

   ....

   ....   (2)

5. What characteristics of the music in this extract are typical of sub-Saharan African instrumental and vocal music? You should make **two** points for each.

   a) Instrumental music: ....

   ....

   b) Vocal music: ....

   ....   (4)

   (Total 13 marks)

46 Area of Study 4: Indian raga, African music and fusions

Question 32

Track 30

Listen to this track **four** times, and answer the following questions.

1. Which of the **three** musical features listed below can be heard in this extract? Put a cross in the correct boxes.

   Diatonic scale ☒   Pentatonic scale ☒   African drumming ☒   Ternary form ☒

   Jhala ☒   Polyrhythms ☒   Monophonic texture ☒   (3)

2. What term describes the musical relationship between the soloist and the other singers at the start?

   .... (1)

3. Describe as precisely as you can the melodic shape of the **second** solo and group phrases that are heard.

   a) Solo: ....

   ....

   b) Group: ....

   .... (4)

4. Describe the rhythm played by the first drum to enter.

   .... (1)

5. Describe as precisely as you can what happens in the drum parts and vocal parts from 00:36 to 01:00. You should make **four** points in your answer.

   ....

   ....

   ....

   .... (4)

   (Total 13 marks)

Question 33

Track 31

Listen to this extract **three** times and answer the questions below.

1. Identify the traditional African instrument you can hear throughout this extract.

   .... (1)

2. Where is this instrument most commonly played? Put a cross in the correct box.

   West Africa ☒   Central Africa ☒   North Africa ☒   (1)

3. What is this instrument made of and how is it played?

   ....

   .... (2)

4. Identify **three** other instruments used in this extract.

   a) .... b) ....

   c) .... (3)

5. There is a bass riff in this extract. What do you understand by the term 'riff'?

   .... (1)

6. For how many bars does the bass riff last? Put a cross in the correct box.

   1 bar ☒   2 bars ☒   3 bars ☒   4 bars ☒   (1)

7. Which **three** words best describe the phrases sung by the male solo vocalist? Put a cross in the correct boxes.

   Ascending ☒   Scalic ☒   Descending ☒   (1)

   Angular ☒   Repetitive ☒   Varied ☒   (3)

8. Which statement best describes the tempo of the extract? Underline your answer.

   The tempo is fairly quick throughout.

   The tempo accelerates slightly towards the end.

   When the voices enter the tempo becomes a little slower.

   The tempo is constantly changing. (1)

   (Total 13 marks)

Fusions

Question 34

Track 32

Listen to this track **five** times and answer the following questions.

1. Underline those words or phrases below which can be used to describe the introduction to this extract.

   Syncopation   Swing rhythms   Trombones   Call and response

   Imperfect cadence   Perfect cadence   Atonal   Trumpets

   Guitars (5)

2. Put a cross next to the correct rhythm of the introduction from the choice below.

   (1)

3. In the chorus (which begins after the introduction, with the words 'Tsutsu tsosemo'), at what interval do the two voices sing? Put a cross in the correct box.

   3rd ☒   4th ☒   6th ☒   Octave ☒ (1)

4. The chorus uses a repeating chord progression in the key of F major. Identify the progression below by putting a cross in the correct box.

   B♭ – Gm – C – F ☒   C – C – F – F ☒

   C – B♭ – C – F ☒   B♭ – C – F – F ☒ (1)

5. Describe **one** way in which the verse (which comes after the chorus) is the same as the chorus, and **one** way in which it is different from the chorus.

   a) Same: ....

   b) Different: .... (2)

6. After the second chorus, which instrument plays a solo?

   .... (1)

7. This extract is an example of 'Highlife' – a fusion of African and Western musical styles. List **two** African and **two** Western characteristics that can be heard in this extract.

   a) African:

   i) ....

   ii) ....

   b) Western:

   i) ....

   ii) .... (4)

   (Total 15 marks)

Question 35

Track 33

This is an extract from Fanshawe's *African Sanctus*, which combines a setting of the Latin Mass with tapes of Fanshawe's own recordings from his journeys around Africa. Listen to it **three** times and answer the questions below.

1. Which percussion instrument plays the two notes heard repeatedly at the start of the extract?

   .... (1)

2. Which term best describes the voices heard at the beginning of this extract? Put a cross in the correct box.

   Mixed choir ☒ Female choir ☒ Male choir ☒ (1)

3. Put a cross next to the word that best describes the texture of the choral singing in this opening section.

   Monophonic ☒ Homophonic ☒ Polyphonic ☒ Heterophonic ☒ (1)

4. What happens to the tempo when the African singing begins?

   .... (1)

5. Put a cross next to **three** terms below which describe music heard in this extract.

   Call and response ☒ Pedal note ☒ Syncopation ☒

   Ground bass ☒ Theme and variations ☒ Polyrhythmic ☒ (3)

6. Describe in as much detail as you can how African and Western music have been combined in this extract.

   ....

   ....

   ....

   .... (4)

   (Total 11 marks)

Question 36

Track 34

Listen to this arrangement of some music from a Bollywood film **four** times, and answer the questions below.

1. What type of drum plays the introduction? Put a cross in the correct box.

   Tabla ☒   Djembe ☒   Bass drum ☒   Dhol ☒   (1)

2. One of the instruments added straight after the introduction is a low-pitched brass instrument called a sousaphone. Notate the rhythm of the one-bar ostinato played by this instrument.

   ‖ 4/4 _____ | (1)

3. Name the two brass instruments that play the call and response phrases in the passage after the introduction (one instrument for each).

   a) Call: ....

   b) Response: ....   (2)

4. Which of these drums is added after the introduction? Put a cross in the correct box.

   Bongo ☒   Timpani ☒   Snare drum ☒   Conga ☒   (1)

5. What new melody instrument do you hear towards the end of the extract? Put a cross in the correct box.

   Clarinet ☒   Soprano saxophone ☒   Violin ☒   Flute ☒   (1)

6. How has bhangra influenced this track?

   .... (1)

   (Total 7 marks)

Glossary

Remember that you are expected to use technical terms correctly and you should be able to identify something when you hear it.

A cappella. Unaccompanied singing (usually choral).

Accent. A note given emphasis, either because of its position, because it is marked with a symbol such as > or *sf*, because it is syncopated, because there is a melodic leap before it and so on.

Additive rhythm. Rhythmic patterns made from repetitions of a fast note-value as opposed to rhythms based on divisions and multiplications of the time value of a regular pulse. Fast quavers grouped 3+3+2 or 3+2+3 (perhaps with an 8/8 time signature) are additive rhythms as opposed to metrical rhythms, such as a minim plus four quavers in 4/4 time.

Agogo. In African music, a double bell (that can produce two pitches) played with a stick.

Air. English or French for 'song'.

Alap. In north-Indian music, an unmetred improvised prelude.

Aleatoric. Determined by chance.

Alto. A high male or low female voice.

Anacrusis. One or more weak-beat notes before the first strong beat of a phrase. Often called a 'pick-up'.

Answering phrase. The second of a pair of balanced phrases that sounds as if it is answering the first phrase (the 'question'). Such symmetrical (or 'periodic') phrases are also known as the antecedent (the question) and the consequent (the answer).

Antiphony. Music in which two or more groups of performers alternate with each other.

Arco. An instruction for a string player to use the bow, rather than playing **pizzicato** or **col legno**.

Aria. A solo vocal work with instrumental accompaniment.

Arpeggio. A chord played as successive rather than simultaneous notes.

Articulation. The length of notes in relation to their context (e.g. **legato** as opposed to **staccato** articulation).

Atonal music, Atonality. Music that is unrelated to a tonic note and so has no sense of key.

Attack. The start-point of a sound. *See also* **Decay**.

Augmentation. A proportionate increase in the note-lengths of a melody, e.g. when two quavers and a crotchet become two crotchets and a minim. The opposite of augmentation is **diminution**.

Backing vocals. Sung parts that accompany the main singer in a pop song.

Balafon. A west-African **xylophone**.

Baroque. The period c. 1600–1750 and its music.

Bass. 1. A low male voice. 2. The lowest-sounding part of a composition whether for voices or instruments.

Basso continuo. In Baroque music, a **bass** part from which accompanying chords (often indicated by **figures**) are improvised on a harmony instrument, such as a harpsichord, organ or lute. The part is also usually played on one or more bass instruments, such as cello, bassoon or double bass.

Beat. The underlying pulse of metrical music.

Bend. *See* **Pitch-bending**.

Bhangra. An amalgamation of western pop styles and traditional Punjabi styles of music.

Binary form. A musical structure in two sections (AB).

Bitonality. The use of two different keys at the same time.

Blue note. *See* **Blues scale**.

Blues. A musical genre that evolved in the USA among former black slaves. It draws on west-African traditions, such as blue notes and call-and-response patterns between singer and a lead instrument (usually guitar), but was also influenced by western folk music.

Blues scale. A scale in which some degrees (**blue notes**) are flattened, most commonly the third and seventh degrees.

Book. The spoken words of a musical, along with directions for staging and lyrics for songs. *See also* **Libretto**.

BPM. Abbreviation of beats per minute.

Break. 1. In pop music and jazz, an instrumental solo (usually improvised). 2. In dance music such as **hip-hop**, a short passage (also known as the 'drop') in which all parts drop out, the gap being filled by sound effects or a brief silence.

Bridge. 1. A contrasting passage (such as a **middle eight**) in a pop song. 2. The structure that transmits vibrations from the strings to the body on instruments such as the violin and guitar.

Britpop. A style of British pop music that evolved in the 1990s, is strongly influenced by guitar-based British pop groups of 30 years earlier.

Broken chord. A chord in which the notes are sounded individually in patterns, rather than together.

Cadence. A point of repose at the end of a phrase, sometimes harmonised with two cadence chords. *See* **Perfect cadence, Imperfect cadence, Plagal cadence** and **Interrupted cadence**.

Cadenza. A florid, free-time solo in an **aria** or **concerto** movement.

Call-and-response. A technique whereby a soloist sings or plays a phrase to which a larger group responds.

Canon. A compositional device in which a melody in one part is repeated in another part while the melody in the first part continues.

Chaal rhythm. Basic rhythm found in **bhangra**.

Chaconne and passacaglia. Though different in their origins, by the 18th century there was little difference between these two forms. Both continuous variations based on an **ostinato** which can be a repeating bass pattern, a harmonic progression or both.

Choir. A group of singers performing together.

Chorus. 1. In popular music, a setting of the refrain of the lyrics. 2. A large group of singers usually performing compositions in several parts. 3. The electronic multiplication of an individual part to give it greater body.

Chromatic notes. *See* **Diatonic and chromatic notes**.

Circle of 5ths. A series of bass notes each a 5th lower or higher than the previous note, though in practice the same pitches are achieved by a part that falls a fifth and rises a fourth alternately. Also used to describe a series of triads or keys with a similar relationship.

Classical. 1. Music of the period c. 1750–1825. 2. In a wider sense, music that is related to learned or historic traditions, such as Indian classical music. 3. In a still broader sense, any type of music that is regarded as 'art music' rather than pop or folk – so styles as varied as Baroque, Romantic, Expressionist and Postmodernist can all be described in a general way as 'classical'.

Coda. A closing section at the end of a movement or song.

Col legno. An instruction for a string player to use the wood, rather than the hair, of the bow.

Coloratura. A very ornamental style of vocal music, especially associated with soprano soloists in some types of opera.

Concerto. A composition for one or more solo instruments accompanied by an **orchestra**. Usually in three movements.

Concord. *See* **Consonance and dissonance**.

Consonance and dissonance. The relative stability (consonance) or instability (dissonance) of two or more notes sounded simultaneously. Consonant intervals and chords are called concords. Dissonant intervals and chords are called discords.

Con sordino. An instruction for a performer to use a mute.

Contrapuntal. A texture that uses **counterpoint**.

Continuo. *See* **Basso continuo**.

Countermelody. A new melody that occurs simultaneously with a melody that has been heard before.

Counterpoint. The simultaneous combination of two or more melodic lines.

Cross-rhythm. A rhythm that conflicts with the regular pattern of beats of a composition, or the combination of two conflicting rhythms within a single beat (e.g. duplets against triplets).

Cyclic. A musical structure in which two or more different movements are linked by the use of the same or similar themes.

Da capo. An instruction to repeat the music from the beginning, usually ending where the word *Fine* occurs in the score.

Decay. The end-part of a sound. A note might decay (get quieter) gradually or it might stop suddenly. *See also* **Attack**.

Decks. Turntables used by DJs.

Decorations. Printed or unprinted embellishments to the written score which enrich a performance and provide variety in repeated passages.

Delay. An audio effect in which sound is replayed after a very short delay. Often it will be played back a number of times in quick succession, giving the effect of a repeating, decaying echo.

Descant. A melodic line sung above the main melody of a hymn or similar vocal piece.

Dhol. A large cylindrical south-Asian drum.

Dhrupad. A traditional style of dignified, slow singing in north-Indian music. *See also* **Khayal**.

Diatonic and chromatic notes. Diatonic notes belong to the scale of the prevailing key while chromatic notes are foreign to it. For example, in C major G is a diatonic note whereas G♯ is a chromatic note.

Diminution. A proportionate decrease in the note-lengths of a melody, e.g. when two quavers and a crotchet become two semiquavers and a quaver. The opposite of diminution is **augmentation**.

Discord. *See* **Consonance and dissonance**.

Dissonance. *See* **Consonance and dissonance**.

DJ. 1. A person who presents and comments on recorded music, typically on the radio. **2.** A performer who creates continuous music for dancing by mixing pre-recorded tracks.

Djembe. Goblet-shaped west-African drum.

Dominant. The fifth degree of a major or minor scale.

Dominant 7th chord. A chord consisting of the dominant – the fifth degree of the scale – plus diatonic notes a 3rd, 5th and 7th above it.

Dotted rhythm. A two-note pattern consisting of a dotted note followed by a note only one-third as long as the dotted note.

Double-stopping. The performance of a two-note chord on a bowed string instrument.

Doubling. The simultaneous performance of a melody by two or more players, either at the same pitch or separated by octaves.

Drone. The same as **pedal**, but the term is usually associated with folk music.

Drum and bass. Very fast popular dance style.

Drum-loop. A short series of drum beats that can be repeated over and over again without any musical of tempo inconsistencies.

Drum machine. A synthesiser capable of simulating the sounds of a number of percussion instruments.

Dundun. A doubled-headed hourglass drum from Africa that can be used as a **talking drum**.

Dynamics. The loudness (f) and quietness (p) of notes and other nuances that affect their volume, for example *cresc.* and *dim.*.

Enharmonics. Two notes of the same pitch that are notated differently, e.g. C♭ and B.

Episode. A distinct section within a movement.

EQ. Abbreviation of equalisation – a signal processing device that alters the frequency responce of a sound.

Expressionism. An early 20th-century style characterized by the expression of inner fears and obsessions, often through distorted or violent artistic ideas.

Falsetto. A special vocal technique that enables a man to sing with a different tone and in a higher register.

Figure. Another name for a motif.

Figured bass. A **bass** part with Arabic numerals indicating the **intervals** above the bass that are to be played in order to form the desired chords.

Fill. In pop music and jazz, a brief improvised flourish (often on drums) to fill the gap between the end of one phrase and the beginning of another.

Filtering. In recording, the process of masking out some components of an electronic signal. For example, a low-pass filter might be used to remove high frequencies from a bass drum sound to give it more of a dull thud.

Flutter-tonguing. On wind instruments, rolling an 'r' with the tongue while blowing to produce rapid repetitions of a note.

Frets. Raised strips running at right angles across the fingerboard of instruments such as the guitar, **lute** and **sitar**.

Funk. A style of pop music that evolved in America in the late 1960s and early 1970s. It developed from **soul**, but is more rhythmic and less mellow, with an emphasis on guitars, drums and punchy brass parts rather than orchestral backings.

Fusion. Music in which two or more styles are blended together, for example **bhangra**.

Gamak. In north-Indian music, approaching a note by sliding to it from the note above or below.

Gankogui. In African music, a double bell (that can produce two pitches) played with a stick.

Garage. A term used in the UK for a type of electronic dance music of the mid-1990s that combined the deep bass of **jungle** with **drum loops** and **rap-like** vocals.

Gat. In north Indian music, an instrumental composition (as opposed to an improvisation).

Genre. A category or group, such as the piano sonata.

Gharana. In north-Indian music, an extended family of musicians learning from a particular master and often living together.

Glissando. A slide from one pitch to another.

Gospel. An emotional style of African-American song using texts that reflect aspects of Protestant evangelical religious experience. The style includes spontaneous often syncopated ornamentation, with blue notes, stamping and clapping, and congregational interjections such as 'Yes Lord'.

Griot. A west-African poet and musician who travels around singing traditional stories.

Ground bass. A melody in the bass part of a composition that is repeated many times and which forms the basis for a continuous set of melodic and/or harmonic **variations**.

Harmonic progression. A series of chords.

Harmonics. On string instruments (including the harp and guitar), very high and pure sounds produced by placing a finger on a string very lightly before plucking or bowing.

Harmonium. A reed organ, once found in churches and now used in some music of the Indian subcontinent.

Harpsichord. A keyboard instrument with one, two or three manuals controlling a set of jacks. Each jack has a quill or piece of plastic that plucks a string when a key is depressed.

Heterophonic. A texture made up of a simple tune and a more elaborate version of it played or sung together.

Hip-hop. A culture that evolved in urban black America in the 1970s. Features include the use of **rap** by an **MC**, with an accompaniment of **looped** drum **breaks** from other songs, created by a **DJ**.

Homophonic. A texture in which one part has all of the melodic interest, while the others provide a simple accompaniment.

Hook. In pop music, a catchy, memorable short melodic idea.

Hosho. A rattle made from a gourd with seeds inside (or beads around), often used to accompany the **mbira** in African music.

Imitation. A **contrapuntal** device in which a melodic idea in one part is copied in another part while the first part continues. Only the opening notes of the original melody need to be repeated to create this effect.

Imperfect cadence. Almost any chord plus chord V at the end of a phrase.

Glossary

Interlude. Music played between sections of a longer piece.

Interrupted cadence. Chord V followed by an unexpected chord (such as VI) at the end of a phrase.

Interval. The distance between two pitches. So, in the scale of C major, the interval between the first and second notes is a 2nd (C–D), the interval between the first and third notes is a 3rd (C–D–E), and so on.

Inversion. 1. The process of turning a melody upside down so that every interval of the original is maintained but moves in the opposite direction. **2.** A chord is inverted when a note other than the root is sounded in the bass. **3.** An interval is inverted when one of the two notes moves an octave so that instead of being below the second note it is above it (or vice versa).

Isicathamiya. A style of unaccompanied choral singing that originated from the Zulu people of South Africa.

Jhala. In north-Indian music, a lively, rhythmical improvised section in fast tempo following the **jhor**.

Jhor. In north Indian music, an improvisatory section that has a strong pulse but no set metre. It is in medium tempo and follows the **alap**.

Jungle. An early name for **drum and bass**.

Key. The relationship between the pitches of notes in which one particular pitch called the tonic seems more important than any other pitch. The pitch of the tonic determines the key of the music.

Khali. In north Indian music, an unaccented **vibhag** in which the first beat is indicated by a wave of the hand rather than a clap.

Khayal. A traditional style of singing in north-Indian music, more florid and improvisatory than **dhrupad**.

Kora. A long-necked harp used in west-African music.

Legato. Notes that are performed smoothly, without gaps between them. The opposite of **staccato**.

Leitmotif. A musical idea, often used in opera and musicals as a reminder of a particular character, setting or situation.

Libretto. The words of an opera or musical. In the case of a musical, the libretto includes both the **book** (the spoken words) and the lyrics (the song words).

Lick. A short solo phrase in pop and jazz.

Lute. A fretted plucked-string instrument popular in the renaissance and baroque periods.

Major and minor. A major interval is greater than a minor interval by a semitone. The interval between the first and third degrees of a major scale is four semitones, one semitone greater than the interval between the same degrees in a minor scale.

Master drum. The drum played by the leader of an African percussion group (the master drummer).

Matra. The term for the 'measure' in which a **tal** is performed.

Mbira. An African 'thumb piano', consisting of metal strips attached to a resonator that are twanged by both thumbs plus, in some regions, the index finger(s).

Meend. In north-Indian music, a type of **gamak** (ornament) involving a smooth glide between notes.

Melismatic. A vocal style in which several notes are sung to the same syllable. The opposite of **syllabic**.

Melodic inversion. *See* **Inversion 1**.

Melody and accompaniment. A type of homophonic texture in which a tune is freely accompanied by other parts.

Metre. The repeating patterns produced by strong and weak pulses, usually of the same duration.

Middle eight. A contrasting section in the middle of a song (not necessarily eight bars long).

MIDI. Musical Instrument Digital Interface: a system for exchanging music performance data between suitably equipped computers and/or electronic instruments.

Minimalism. A style of the late 20th century. It was a reaction to the complexities of modernist styles and is characterised by the varied repetition of simple rhythmic, melodic or harmonic ideas.

Minor. *See* **Major and minor**.

Minuet. An elegant dance in $\frac{3}{4}$, it was the only dance of the Baroque suite to be retained in Classical instrumental music where where it forms a **ternary** structure with a **trio** (minuet–trio–minuet).

Mixing. The process of blending separate sound sources.

Modal music. Music based on one of the scales of seven pitch classes commonly found in western music, but excluding the major and minor scales.

Modernism. A cultural movement of the early 20th century that rejected tradition in order to create new and sometimes startling forms of expression. Complexity and the free use of dissonance are features of much modernist music. *See also* **Postmodernism**.

Modulation. The process by which music changes one key.

Monophonic. A texture consisting of a single unaccompanied melody which may be performed by a soloist or by many people playing or singing the melody in unison or in octaves.

Mordent. An ornament consisting of rapid movement from a main pitch to an adjacent pitch and back.

Motif. A short melodic or rhythmic idea that is sufficiently distinctive to allow it to be modified, manipulated and possibly combined with other motifs while retaining its own identity.

Multi-tracking. A recording technique where several tracks of sound are recorded independently but can be played back together.

Note-row. *See* **Tone-row**.

Octave. The interval between the first and last degrees of an eight-note major or minor scale. The two notes forming this interval are 12 semitones apart and have the same letter name.

Octave displacement. The practice of moving notes of a **tone-row** one or more octaves from their original pitches, thus producing the angular melodic lines that are typical of most serial compositions.

On-beat and off-beat notes. Notes articulated on strong and weak beats of the bar respectively.

Orchestra. A large instrumental ensemble that includes string players, and often woodwind, brass and percussion sections. A full-size symphony orchestra usually has at least 60 players. Smaller groups are often called chamber orchestras. A string orchestra consists only of violins, violas, cellos and double basses.

Ornamentation. Decorative notes in a melody.

Ostinato. A rhythmic, melodic or harmonic pattern repeated many times in succession. Often called a **riff** in pop music.

Outro. In pop music and jazz, a closing section – the opposite of an intro. An outro is essentially the same as a **coda**, although a fade-out ending is more likely to be termed an outro than a coda.

Pakhawaj. A large wooden cylindrical drum in north-Indian music. It has skins at both ends and is played with the palms and fingers.

Palta. In north-Indian music, a scalic melodic pattern practised to improve technique on the sitar.

Pan. A control that determines the position (from extreme left to extreme right) of a sound in the stereo field.

Passacaglia. *See* **Chaconne and passacaglia**.

Passing note. A non-harmony note that moves by step between two harmony notes.

Pause. An extension of a note or rest beyond its normal length, causing a temporary interruption of the underlying pulse.

Pedal. A sustained or repeated note sounded against changing harmony.

Pentatonic music. Music based on a scale of five notes.

Perfect cadence. Chord V followed by chord I at the end of phrase.

Phasing, phase-shifting. A technique common in Minimalist music, in which a melody in one part is copied by another part in a slightly extended or curtailed version. As the two parts loop their respective patterns, they get increasingly out of step and then gradually move back into phase, when they once again coincide.

Phrase structure. The length and pattern of melodic phrases that make up a section of music. For example, the verse of a song might have a structure of four four-bar phrases in the pattern ABAC.

Pitch. The height or depth of a note. This can be relative and expressed as an **interval** between two notes, or it can be an absolute quality determined by the number of vibrations per second of a string, a column of air or a membrane.

Pitch-bending. Detuning a note so it slides to another pitch.

Pizzicato. An instruction for a player of a bowed string instrument to pluck the strings rather than to bow them. *See also* **Arco**.

Plagal cadence. Chord IV followed by chord I at the end of a phrase.

Polyphonic. A texture made up of two or more different melodies sounding together. Today the term polyphony and **counterpoint** are used interchangeably.

Polyrhythm. The simultaneous combination of two or more distinctly different and often conflicting types of rhythm.

Portamento. A slide from one pitch to another. Often the same as glissando, but the term portamento is preferred by singers.

Postmodernism. A late-20th century reaction to the **modernism** of much music in the first half of the century. Post modernism is characterized by simple but novel structures and mainly diatonic harmony. It includes **Minimalism**, new styles of religious music, and cross-over fusions that combine elements of pop, jazz and world music with contemporary classical music.

Power chord. A loud guitar chord consisting of an open 5th (the root and 5th of a triad, without a 3rd).

Primary triads. Chords I, IV and V.

Programme music. Music meant to suggest visual images or a story.

Pulse. Beat.

Pulsing. A technique used in **Minimalism**, involving numerous rapid repetitions of the same chord.

Quantisation. On a **sequencer**, the process of automatically adjusting data to fit within defined limits. Commonly used to shift note-starts to (or nearer to) their rhythmically exact positions, it can also be used to modify note-lengths and velocity levels.

R&B, Rhythm and blues. A style of black American music combining elements of jazz and blues which emerged in the 1940s. More recently R&B is also used to describe urban – a combination of soul and hip-hop originating in the 1980s.

Rag (raga). A pattern of ascending and descending notes associated with particular moods and used as the basis for melodic improvisation in Indian classical music.

Range. The distance between the lowest and highest notes of a melody or composition, or between the highest and lowest notes that can be played on an instrument or sung by a vocalist.

Rap. A style of African-American music that first emerged during the late 1970s. Its performers use semi-spoken rhythms over backing tracks created using **DJ** techniques and sampling.

Rasa. In north Indian music, the emotional character of a piece.

Recapitulation. The repetition of music heard earlier in the same movement, notably a movement in sonata form.

Refrain. A melody or passage of music repeated at intervals throughout a work, most commonly found in folk and pop music.

Register. A part of the range of a voice or instrument. The lowest pitches of a clarinet are in the chalumeau register. The highest pitches of a Baroque trumpet are in the clarino register.

Relative major, Relative minor. Keys that share the same key signature, such as G major and E minor.

Reprise. The return of a section of music. In a musical, a reprise is often designed to give the audience a chance to enjoy again some or all of a popular number heard earlier.

Retrograde. A series of note values, pitches or chords played backwards.

Retrograde inversion. A series of notes played backwards and upside down.

Reverb. Abbreviation of reverberation. The complex series of reflections that occurs when sound is made in an enclosed space. Digitally produced reverb is often added to recordings.

Riff. In jazz, pop and rock, a short, memorable melodic pattern repeated many times in succession. *See also* **Ostinato**.

Ritornello. An instrumental section in a Baroque aria, or a section for a large string ensemble in a Baroque concerto. In some arias and movements the same or similar musical materials are used in every appearance of the ritornello (like the refrain of a rondo).

Romantic. In music, the period c. 1825–1900.

Rondo. A composition in which a passage at the start is repeated several times at intervals throughout the work, the repeats being separated from each other by contrasting passages called episodes.

Root. In tonal music, the fundamental pitch of any chord built from superimposed thirds.

Rubato. Expressive changes to the position of beats within a bar, sometimes leading to fluctuations in the overall tempo. A common performance technique in some types of romantic music.

Sam. In north Indian music, the first beat of a **tal**.

Sampler. A device for recording sections of sound (samples), which allows them to be played back with various modifications (e.g. at different speeds, in a loop or in combination with other samples).

Sarangi. In north-Indian music, a fretless bowed instrument with three main strings and a range of other strings that vibrate in sympathy with them.

Sargam. In north-Indian music, a system for naming notes, comparable with sol-fa (do, re, me and so on) in western music.

Sarod. A north-Indian plucked-string instrument with a number of melody strings, **drone** strings and **sympathetic strings**. Unlike the **sitar** it has a metal fingerboard and no **frets**.

Scalic, scalar. Adjectives referring to a melodic contour in which adjacent notes move by step in a similar manner to notes in a scale.

Scherzo. A fast movement usually in triple time, often used as a middle movement in 19th-century instrumental music, alternating with a **trio** to form a **ternary** structure (scherzo–trio–scherzo).

Score. A written document representing how a piece of music should be played or how it was played.

Scotch snap. A two-note rhythm consisting of a short on-beat note followed by a long off-beat note (e.g. an on-beat semiquaver followed by an off-beat dotted quaver).

Scratching. The technique of manipulating a vinyl record in order to repeat a passage of music several times.

Semitone. The interval between two adjacent pitches on a keyboard instrument (including black notes).

Sequence. 1. The immediate repetition of a motif or phrase of a melody in the same part but at a different pitch. A harmonic progression can be treated in the same way. **2.** Performance data stored by a sequencer.

Sequencer. Computer software (or more rarely a purpose-built electronic device) for the input, editing and playback of music performance data using MIDI.

Serial music, serialism. Music based on manipulations of a series of 12 notes including every pitch of a chromatic scale.

Series. *See* **Tone-row**.

Setting. Music added to a text so that the words are sung instead of spoken.

Seventh chord. A triad plus a note a 7th above the root. The dominant 7th consists of a major triad on the fifth degree of the scale (e.g. G–B–D in C major) plus a minor 7th above the root (F). In the same key the tonic 7th consists of a major triad on the first degree of the scale (C–E–G) plus a major 7th above the root (B).

Sforzando (*sf*). Strongly accented.

Simple metre. A metre in which each beat can be divided into two shorter notes of equal length. $\frac{3}{4}$ is a simple triple metre – there are three crotchet beats, each consisting of two quavers.

Sitar. A north-Indian fretted plucked-string instrument, with a number of melody strings, **drone** strings and **sympathetic** strings.

Solo. 1. A performance by a single musician. **2.** A piece of music or a passage of music written for a single musician.

Soprano. A high female or unbroken boy's voice.

Soul. A style of pop muic that evolved in America in the late 1950s. It is a combination of **R&B** and **gospel**, and places emphasis on vocalists and the merging of religious and secular themes.

Sprechstimme (speech-voice), Sprechgesang (speechsong). A type of vocal production halfway between singing and speaking.

Stab. In pop music, a single accented chord, played staccato by brass (real or synthesised) or by using an orchestral sample.

56 Glossary

Staccato. Notes that are performed shorter than printed so that each is detached from its neighbours. Often shown in notation by dots above or below the notes affected. The opposite of **legato**.

Stave. A set of parallel lines on which pitches are notated.

String quartet. A chamber music group consisting of two violins, a viola and a cello.

Strophic song. A song in which every verse uses the same music.

Subdominant. The fourth degree of a major or minor scale.

Subito. Suddenly, e.g. subito *p* – suddenly quiet.

Suite. A collection of pieces intended to be performed together.

Swing quavers, swung quavers. The division of the beat into pairs of notes in which the first is longer than the second. In music notation this approximates to the pattern ♩♪.

Syllabic. A vocal style in which each syllable is set to its own note. The opposite of **melismatic**.

Symmetrical phrase. *See* **Answering phrase**.

Sympathetic string. A string that is not played but resonates 'in sympathy' with strings of the same note which are played.

Symphony. As most often used today, an orchestral composition, often in four movements.

Syncopation. Accentuation of notes sounded off the beat or on a weak beak, often with rests on some of the strong beats.

Synthesiser. An electronic instrument that can produce and modify sound. It can be used to imitate other musical instruments and to produce non-musical sounds.

Tabla. **1.** In Indian music, a pair of drums played with hands and fingers by a single performer. **2.** The smaller drum of this pair (the larger being called a baya).

Tal, tala, talam. A cyclic rhythmic pattern in Indian music that forms the basis for improvisation.

Talking drums. In Africa, drums on which sounds similar to elements of speech can be used for wordless communication.

Tan. In north Indian music, improvised fast variations that expand the basic notes of a **rag**.

Tanpura, tambura. A type of Indian plucked-string instrument with four drone strings.

Tape-loop. A section of magnetic tape fixed end to end so that the same music can be repeated indefinitely. The process is now usually accomplished using a digital sequencer.

Techno. A style of 1980s **sequencer**-based electronic dance music, with few or no vocals. Its main emphasis is on intricate drum tracks, samples and effects, rather than on melodic material, chord changes or strong bass parts.

Tempo. The speed of the underlying beat.

Tenor. A male voice higher than a bass, but lower than an alto.

Ternary form. A three-part structure (ABA) in which the first and last sections are identical or very similar. These enclose a contrasting central section.

Tessitura. The part of a pitch range in which a passage of music mainly lies.

Texture. The number and timbres of parts in a composition and the way they relate to each other.

Theka. In north Indian music, the pattern of drum strokes that make up a **tal**.

Theme. A main idea in a conception – usually a melody. One of the main ideas in a composition, but it could, for example, be a chord progression. *See also* **Variations**.

Through-composed. A song in which each verse has different music.

Tierce de Picardie. A major 3rd in the final tonic chord of a minor-key passage.

Tihai. In north Indian music, a **tabla** pattern that is played three times (usually ending on **sam**) to mark the end of a section.

Timbre (pronounced tam-bruh). Tone colour. The clarinet has a different timbre from the trumpet, but the clarinet also has different timbres in various parts of its **range**. Timbre can also be affected by the way an instrument is played, for example by using a mute or plucking a string instead of using the bow.

Time-line. In west African drumming, a short repeated rhythm that guides the other players. It may be clapped or played on an instrument such as an **agogo**.

Tintal (pronounced teen-tal). In north-Indian music, one of the most common types of **tal**, consisting of 16 beats shaped as four patterns of four.

Tonal language. A language in which the pitch level of the speaking voice helps to determine the meaning of the words.

Tonal music. Music in a clearly defined key. A key is established by the relationships between the pitches derived from major and minor scales. The most important relationship is that between the tonic (the first degree of a scale) and all other pitches.

Tone. **1.** An interval of two semitones, e.g. C–D. **2.** A sound of definite pitch. **3.** The timbre of a particular instrument or voice.

Tone-row. A series of 12 different pitch classes. In strict **serialism** none of these pitch classes is repeated until all 12 have been used.

Tonic. The first degree of a **major** or **minor** scale.

Transformation. **1.** A compositional technique in which a melody, rhythm or chord progression is changed so it takes on a new character. The process was used by a number of Romantic composers and is common in Minimalist music. **2.** In serial music, a different version of the prime order of a note row, such as an **inversion** or a **transposition**.

Transposition. The performance or notation of a passage of music or of a whole piece at a pitch level lower or higher than the original.

Treble. A boy's unbroken voice.

Tremolo. The continuous rapid repetition of either a single pitch or two alternating pitches more than a tone apart.

Triad. A chord of three pitches consisting of a bass note and notes a 3rd and a 5th above it.

Trill. An ornament (often shown as *tr*) consisting of the rapid alternation of two pitches a step apart.

Trio. **1.** Music for three solo performers. **2.** Music for one performer written throughout in three contrapuntal parts. **3.** The middle section of the minuet–trio–minuet (or scherzo–trio–scherzo) third movement of many Classical symphonies and string quartets.

Triplet. A group of three notes of equal length played in the time of two notes of the same time value.

Tritone. An interval of three tones, e.g. F–B.

Turn. A four-note ornament that starts a step above the written note, drops to the written note, then drops to the step below and finally returns to the written note.

Tutti. A passage in which all or most of the members of an ensemble are playing.

Twelve-bar blues. A structure that originated in **blues** which has been widely adopted in jazz and pop music. The melody consists of three four-bar phrases, the second often being a repeat of the first. The chord structure is built around chords I and IV and often takes the form I–I–I–I IV–IV–I–I V–IV–I–I (one chord per bar). Other patterns are possible (such as V–V–I–I for the last four bars) and chords are frequently decorated with 7ths or other additions.

Twelve-tone music. *See* **Serial music**.

Unison. The combined sound of two or more notes of the same pitch.

Variations. A musical structure in which a theme is repeated, each time with alterations to one or more of its original elements.

Verse-and-chorus. A standard form used in popular song in which a chorus is repeated after each verse. Sometimes an instrumental break or a middle eight is featured.

Verticalisation. In serial music, the use of adjacent notes from a tone row as a chord.

Vibhag. In north-Indian music, one of the groups of beats that makes up a **tal**.

Virtuoso. A performer of outstanding technical ability.

Word-painting. The illustration in music of the meaning or suggestion of particular words or phrases in a text.

Xylophone. A percussion instrument in which beaters are used to strike a set of tuned wooden bars.